ALIEN ENCOUNTERS

ALIEN ENCOUNTERS

Written and Illustrated by Peter A. Campbell

The Millbrook Press • Brookfield, Connecticut

To my brother Paul, whose boyhood passion and extensive library on the UFO phenomenon helped make this book a reality. And to my friend Chris Roe, whose input, humor, and encouragement have not been forgotten.

Also Kathy Silvestri and Thom Valentino who helped bring the words and pictures to life.

But especially to my family: Karen, Seth, Jeremy, and Brendan.

Published by The Millbrook Press, Inc.
2 Old New Milford Road
Brookfield, Connecticut 06804
www.millbrookpress.com

Library of Congress Cataloging-in-Publication data
Campbell, Peter A.
    Alien encounters / written and illustrated by Peter A. Campbell.
    p. cm
    Includes index.
    Summary: A scrapbook of eight well-known alien encounters, using first-hand descriptions to provide illustrations of what the aliens and their spacecraft might have looked like.
    ISBN 0-7613-1402-4 (lib. bdg.)
    1. Unidentified flying objects—Sightings and encounters—Juvenile literature.
(1. Unidentified flying objects. 2. Extraterrestrial beings.
3. Human-alien encounters.)   I. Title.
TL789.2.C36   2000
001.942–dc21   99-25360
                                                              CIP AC

Cover illustration: *sighting Blenheim, New Zealand, 1959*

Contents

Introduction

Since biblical times, the subject of encounters with alien beings from other worlds has fascinated people. Accounts of mysterious visitors descending from starry skies in winged chariots and phantom aerial ships can be found in the myths, legends, drawings, and folklore of many ancient civilizations.

Not until the twentieth century did people begin recording and documenting UFOs (Unidentified Flying Objects), a term adopted by the United States Air Force in 1951 to describe alien encounters.

In 1947 the UFO phenomenon gained momentum in the United States when pilot Kenneth Arnold spotted nine shimmering disc-shaped objects flying in formation as he flew his single-engine plane over the Cascade Mountains of Washington. Pilot Arnold estimated that the UFOs were flying at a speed of almost 1,700 miles (2700 kilometers) per hour.

Shortly after this well-publicized UFO sighting, reports of other such encounters began to surface in newspapers and magazines around the world.

Some reports included stories of flying saucers that appeared in broad daylight over large cities as thousands of people watched. Others tell of UFO crashes and recovered alien bodies. But the most fascinating stories by far are those that describe close encounters with alien beings from another world. Wild claims of strange creatures appearing in all shapes and forms—from large and small aliens with huge heads and big, catlike eyes to robotlike creatures that make odd buzzing sounds, to strange humanlike beings that fly – have fascinated people for years.

Are these stories true? Have people really had contact with alien beings? Have people spoken to visitors from far-off planets? Do the United States military forces actually have UFOs and aliens in their possession?

This book documents eight incredible tales of UFO and alien encounters from 1953 to 1973. Are they true events or just clever hoaxes? The witnesses, people like you and me, from all walks of life, believe strongly that they have had an encounter with an alien being from outer space.

You be the judge.

Kingman, Arizona

May 21, 1953

On an evening in May 1953, a fiery object hurtling down from the sky crashed into the cool desert sand near Kingman, Arizona.

Twenty years later, in 1973, Fritz Werner*, who had been assigned to the Air Material Command Installation Division at the Atomic Proving Ground in Nevada, confirmed in a signed affidavit that the metallic object that had crashed into the Arizona desert was a "flying saucer."

Werner went on to explain that on the afternoon of May 21, a group of approximately fifteen U.S. Air Force specialists boarded a military bus with black-painted windows and departed from Phoenix, Arizona, to an unknown destination.

Upon arrival at the unspecified locale, a roll call of the Air Force specialists was taken, and each man was escorted from the bus.

Situated on the desert ahead of them, illuminated by large floodlights, stood a large oval-shaped metallic object made up of two deep saucerlike parts.

A military police officer escorted Werner through a circle of soldiers who had assembled around the object. Werner's instructions were clear and simple: Determine how fast the strange metallic object had been traveling when it crashed into the desert.

As Werner studied the construction of the odd silvery metal object before him, he became increasingly convinced that it could not have been built anywhere on earth – that it was, for all intents and purposes, a UFO.

Shortly after completing his investigation of the UFO, Werner passed a tent located just a short distance from the spacecraft. Inside the tent was the body of one of the UFO's crew members. The body resembled that of a human being clad in a silver metallic suit.

Later in the day, as the Air Force specialists reboarded the bus to leave, each man was ordered to take an oath, pledging never to disclose to anyone what he had seen that day.

Earlier that same day, eight disc-shaped objects had been spotted in the skies over Prescott, Arizona, 100 miles (160 kilometers) from the Kingman crash site.

*The crash was first reported in 1976 by Raymond Fowler in the April issue of Official UFO magazine. Fowler used the pseudonym "Fritz Werner" to protect the U.S. Air Force officer.

Location of sighting:

The desert northeast of Kingman, Arizona (not far from the Atomic Proving Ground in Nevada).

Witnesses:

U.S. Air Force officer Fritz Werner, approximately thirty U.S. Air Force specialists, and a large number of military police on May 21, 1953.

Craft

Descriptions of UFO:

The surface of the UFO appeared to be a dull silver metal, similar to brushed aluminum. Two deep saucer-shaped objects, one inverted atop the other, formed an oval spherelike construction.* The spacecraft was positioned at a slight angle and embedded in about 25 inches (63 centimeters) of sand. The UFO bore no dents, marks, or scratches and was in perfect condition. A rim, with slotlike openings, circled the center of the spacecraft. The UFO's size was approximately 30 feet (9 meters) in diameter with a convex surface, and it stood 23 feet (7 meters) high from top to bottom. Reports indicated that two swivel chairs were seen inside the spacecraft along with instrument panels.

*Numerous reports of saucer-shaped UFOs, similar to the one discovered in the desert near Kingman, Arizona, were sighted all over the world during the 1950s. The most famous of all – Roswell – took place in 1947.

Alien

The humanlike body of the alien crew member found in the spacecraft was observed lying on a cart in a tent near the UFO. The alien wore a silver metallic suit and a skullcap made of the same material as his outfit. Reports indicated that the alien appeared to have been killed on impact.

Height: 4 feet (122 centimeters)

Body: Dark brown skin
(skin could have been burned or discolored during the crash)

Head and Facial Features:

Eyes: Two   **Nose:** One   **Ears:** Two

Mouth: Small and round

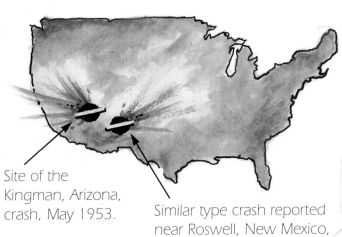

Site of the Kingman, Arizona, crash, May 1953.

Similar type crash reported near Roswell, New Mexico, on July 4, 1947. This site is located about 600 miles (966 kilometers) from Kingman, Arizona.

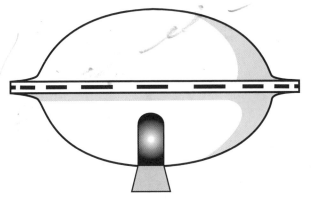

Ground view of saucer with an open hatch door [3-1/2 feet (107 centimeters) high by 1-1/2 feet (46 centimeters) wide] located on the front end of the UFO. Werner also reported seeing a light through the open hatch of the crashed UFO.

Hopkinsville, Kentucky

August 21, 1955

The Sutton farm, located in the peaceful settlement of Kelly in Hopkinsville, Kentucky, is the site of the only known gun battle with creatures from another world.

At 7:00 P.M. on the evening of August 21, 1955, Billy Ray Taylor strolled out to his well for a cool drink of water. Within moments, his attention was drawn skyward to a glowing circular object making its way slowly down to a field beyond the family barn.

Quickly, Billy Ray returned to the house to describe what he had seen to the other members of the Sutton family. His description of a glowing spaceship landing in a nearby field was met with disbelief.

Everyone in the family felt that the spaceship he described was most likely a shooting star.

At 8:00 P.M., a small creature appeared from behind the barn. As it slowly made its way toward the Sutton home, the family dogs began to bark alerting the family of approaching danger.

Hearing the dogs bark and expecting trouble, two of the men quickly grabbed their rifles and cautiously stepped outside to investigate the noise.

Standing 3-1/2 feet (107 centimeters) high, just 60 feet (18 meters) from the house, stood a strange creature. Slowly, with its long thin arms and clawlike hands raised high above its large head, the creature advanced toward the men.

Now, Lucky Sutton could clearly see the alien's face. Its eyes were large and set far apart. A huge pair of ears, elephantlike in appearance, stood out on either side of its moon-shaped head, and its mouth, which was just a slitlike opening, appeared to stretch from ear to ear.

Without hesitation, Billy Ray Taylor and Lucky Sutton raised their guns and fired at the alien creature, knocking it to the ground. Much to their surprise, the alien quickly stood up and scurried into the nearby woods.

Stunned by their discovery, they returned to the house. Gathering the terrified members of the Sutton family together in one room, they quickly turned off the lights.

Suddenly, a piercing scream shattered the stillness of the darkened room. One of the women, frozen in fear, stood pointing a finger in the direction of the screen door at the front of the house. There, on the porch, stood the alien creature staring in at the terrified family.

Another roaring blast from a shotgun sent the alien hurtling backward, but again with no effect as the alien quickly rebounded to its feet.

Immediately, the sound of footsteps could be heard atop the roof. Members of the Sutton family realized that there were more aliens outside their home.

For three hours, gunshot after gunshot rang out into the darkness as creatures fell from the rooftop and treetops that surrounded the farm.

By 11:00 P.M. that evening, the creatures had retreated into the woods. The Sutton family, weary of their long battle with the aliens, hurriedly piled into the family car and fled to the nearest town.

Deputy Sheriff G. Batt, along with two state policemen, returned with Sutton family members to the farmhouse only to discover neither signs of alien creatures nor their spacecraft.

But the nightmare wasn't over. The aliens reappeared about 2:30 A.M. drawing more rifle fire from the Suttons. Finally they left at about 5:30 A.M.

After a thorough investigation of the incident, Chief of Police Russell Greenwell asserted, "Something scared those people – something beyond reason."

It seemed that the aliens were everywhere. This one had climbed on to the porch roof. A blast from one of the Sutton's rifles knocked it to the ground.

Location of sighting:
Kelly, a small settlement near Hopkinsville, Kentucky

Witnesses:
Billy Ray Taylor, during a visit to the Sutton farm in Kelly near Hopkinsville, Kentucky. At 7:00 P.M., August 21,1955, Taylor spotted a bright object descending from the sky to a location behind the Sutton family barn. Eleven Sutton family members were present.

Craft

Descriptions of UFO:
A large and shiny object that discharged a rainbow-colored exhaust

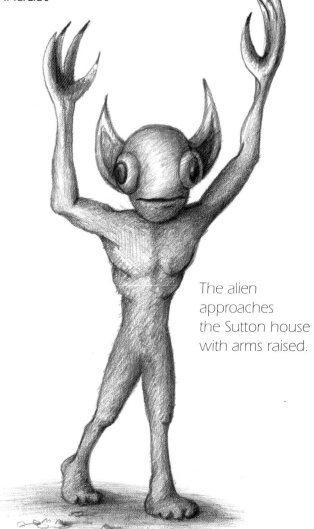

The alien approaches the Sutton house with arms raised.

Alien

Though no one is certain how many aliens surrounded the Sutton farmhouse, members of the Sutton family believe that there were three.

Height: 3-1/2 feet
(107 centimeters)

Body: Either flesh or a spacesuit that emitted a silver metallic glow. Rifle bullets said to have struck the body produced a sound as if having hit a metal object. Appendages of the alien were very long, resembling arms with claw-like hands. When standing upright, the alien's hands almost touched the ground.

Head and facial features:

Head: Large and round, disproportionate with the rest of the body

Eyes: Yellow and set wide apart

Ears: Elephantlike in appearance

Mouth: Slitlike opening extending across the face from ear to ear

Effect of weapons on aliens:
A shotgun and .22-caliber rifle were fired at the aliens by the Suttons. Although close to fifty shots were fired, no damage was caused to the aliens.

Lancaster, New Hampshire

September 19, 1961

Heading homeward in their 1957 Chevrolet Bel Air, which had taken them safely from their home in Portsmouth, New Hampshire, to Niagara Falls and into Quebec, Betty and Barney Hill were happily rounding out a leisurely four-day vacation.

At about 9:00 A.M. on September 19, having cleared customs at the U.S.-Canadian border, the Hills' headed due south along U.S. Highway 3.

Just south of Lancaster, Betty Hill was distracted by something unusual in the clear night sky. A flickering object – like a brilliant star – hovered just below and to the left of the moon. Casually, Betty called Barney's attention to the strange bright object.

As their car moved closer to where the object hovered in the evening sky, Betty could clearly make out its disc-shaped form surrounded by a band of rotating multicolored lights, and two red lights were visible at opposite ends of the UFO.

Eager to get a better look, Barney drove the car to the side of the road. Stepping out from the vehicle into the night air, Barney paused to stare up as the object hovered soundlessly above him.

Large in size with a pancake shape and windows that curved around its entire perimeter, the mysterious object held him in awe. Barney grabbed his binoculars and raised them to his eyes for a closer look. Almost immediately his binoculars honed in on a humanlike figure standing near one of the spacecraft windows.

Barney went numb as the figure in the window slowly turned to gaze in his direction. From his view of the creature through binoculars, Barney could see that the figure had slanted eyes and wore a uniform. Beside the alien stood several crew members who appeared to be operating levers at a control panel.

Fearing that he and Betty might be in danger of capture by these other alien visitors, Barney dropped his binoculars and shouted to Betty to return to the car.

Quickly, the Hills' returned to their car and hastily sped down the road. Within minutes, Barney and Betty spied an intense red light in the road before them. Reducing his speed, Barney caught sight of six humanlike figures standing in the middle of the road.

Suddenly, the car engine sputtered and fell silent as the strange beings began approaching the car. Slowly, the car door swung open. The humanlike creatures with large cat eyes escorted Barney and Betty toward their spacecraft. The Hills' were led up a ramp into the UFO, where they were separated and each taken into a triangular-shaped room where they underwent an examination by the aliens.

Following the examinations, Barney and Betty were taken back to their vehicle. As the Hills stood motionless outside their Chevy, the alien spacecraft vaulted into the sky and in a matter of seconds was lost among the stars.

It wasn't until the Hills' underwent time-regression hypnosis, nearly 2 years later, that they realized they had been abducted by aliens.

The abduction of Barney and Betty Hill was the first case of its kind to receive worldwide attention. Since 1961, thousands of people have reported similar alien encounters and abductions.

Up close the Betty and Barney Hill UFO appeared circular in shape. When viewed at a distance it seemed to take on a cigar or elliptical shape

Location of sighting:
Highway 3, south of Lancaster,
New Hampshire, in a field just off
the highway, a few miles north of
North Woodstock

Witnesses/Abductees:
Postal dispatcher Barney Hill, age 39,
and his wife, Betty Hill, 41, a social
worker, both residents of Portsmouth,
New Hampshire

Craft

Descriptions of UFO:

A circular disc the size of a large aircraft with a row of illuminated windows visible along the edge of the spacecraft. Two red lights were located at opposite ends of the UFO, which could be entered by way of a ramp.

Interior of UFO:

Within the UFO, there was a corridor that followed the curvature of the ship. Separate, triangular-shaped rooms were located off the corridor. An examination table was located in the center of each room. A machine with many wires was brought over to a table where Betty Hill was examined. She later believed a pregnancy test had been performed on her. After the examination, Betty was shown a star map by the alien leader.

Alien leader

Alien crew members

Alien

Barney and Betty Hill reported that they were abducted by six aliens who stood in a road blocking the path of their car.

Height: 5 feet (152 centimeters)

Body: Aliens had oversized chests, and their skin was gray in color. They wore dark uniforms with short jackets. A cap was worn by the alien leader. Slip-on boots covered the aliens' feet. The leader alien wore a black scarf around his neck.

Head and facial features:

Head: Large in proportion to the rest of the body

Eyes: Large, dark-colored catlike eyes that extended to the right and left sides of the head

Nose: None; only two small slitlike openings visible

Mouth: A slitlike aperture with no lips

Socorro, New Mexico

April 24, 1964

At approximately 5:50 P.M. on April 24, 1964, a black Chevrolet made its way through the little town of Socorro, New Mexico.

Exceeding the speed limit, the Chevrolet was soon spotted by on-duty veteran patrolman Lonnie Zamorra, who quickly put the gas pedal of his cruiser to the floor in pursuit of the speeding vehicle making its way north on U.S. Highway 85.

Racing up the highway, Zamorra was suddenly distracted by a roaring sound. Looking up, he spotted a blue flame a half-mile (nearly a kilometer) away in the direction of an old dynamite shack. Abandoning pursuit of the black Chevrolet, Zamorra drove his cruiser to the side of the road to investigate the scene.

Driving slowly along the rough terrain, Zamorra noticed a shiny object just 150 yards (137 meters) away from his location. Alongside a strange-looking object stood two figures the size of young boys. They were clad in white outfits.

As Zamorra approached, the two figures jumped, startled by his sudden appearance. Aware of him now, both creatures turned to look in his direction.

Momentarily ceasing his investigation, Zamorra radioed police headquarters for assistance. He then drove toward the gully where he believed the shiny object was located.

Leaving his cruiser, Zamorra walked in the direction of the odd-looking object ahead of him. As he approached the object, he could clearly make out its form. It was shaped like an egg and white in color, and Zamorra noticed that the UFO had no windows. On the side of the spacecraft was a red insignia that looked like a pyramid within an arch.

The two figures Zamorra had spotted earlier were nowhere in sight.

Within moments, a blue-orange flame exploded at the base of the UFO. Zamorra dove for cover, then watched the spacecraft slowly ascend from the ground. When the space vehicle had reached a height of approximately 20 feet (6 meters), the flame vanished, and the UFO headed in a southwesterly direction at incredible speed.

Within seconds, state patrolman Sam Chavez arrived at the scene to find Zamorra visibly shaken. Confused and upset by what he had witnessed, Zamorra led Chavez toward the area where the UFO had stood just moments before his arrival. Chavez noticed four indentations on the surface of the ground, imprints he believed were made by the spacecraft's landing gear. A smoldering greenwood bush and clumps of singed grass gave further indications of where the UFO had been.

In the time following Zamorra's UFO sighting, he learned that he wasn't the only person to see the spacecraft. At 6:00 P.M. on the same day he sighted the UFO, a family driving north on Highway 85 witnessed a strange object pass directly over their car. The family then noticed a police cruiser leaving the road in pursuit of the UFO.

As Patrolman Zamorra approached the UFO,
a flame exploded from its base.
Startled, he dove for cover.

Location of sighting:
Socorro, New Mexico, located just 50 miles (80 kilometers) from the White Sands Proving Grounds

Witnesses:
Veteran Socorro police officer Lonnie Zamorra, age 31; a family of five (who also observed Zamorra's police cruiser) traveling north on Highway 85, and two men driving on Highway 60 at about the same time that Zamorra was seen in pursuit of the UFO.

Craft

This insignia (as first drawn by Patrolman Zamorra) appeared on the side of the UFO.

Descriptions of UFO:
An oval object with an aluminumlike surface. In the sunlight, the spacecraft appeared to be white. The object had no windows, but a red insignia, resembling a pyramid within an arch, was located on one side of the vehicle. Patrolman Zamorra couldn't see a way to enter or exit the object but assumed that a door or hatch was somewhere on the other side of the UFO just out of his view. The UFO had landing gear that left four wedgelike marks in the hard soil where it had stood.

Height: Approximately 6 to 7 feet (183 to 213 centimeters)

Length: 18 feet (5-1/2 meters)

The four wedge-shaped marks, believed to be made by the UFO's landing gear, were visible on the desert soil where the spacecraft had stood.

Alien

Height: Size of a young boy, approximately 3 feet (90 centimeters)

Body: Figures dressed in white suits; no visible headgear worn

"Mothman," West Virginia

1966 through 1967

In November 1966, UFO sightings in the skies over the western edge of West Virginia began increasing at an alarming rate. About the same time, one of the best-documented and most bizarre creature sightings was reported in the sleepy community of Point Pleasant, West Virginia. A strange birdlike monster with glowing red eyes was reported terrorizing local residents.

On November 15, 1966, near an abandoned World War II ammunition dump known as the TNT area, 7 miles (11 kilometers) outside Point Pleasant, a strange bird-like creature was reported seen by residents.

Two young couples, Mr. and Mrs. Roger Scarberry and Mr. and Mrs. Steve Mallette, were driving past the deserted power plant located on TNT grounds, when they spotted a mysterious-looking figure standing alongside the road, illuminated by the car's headlights. Roger Scarberry could clearly see a pair of large wings tucked against both sides of the motionless creature. Two large glowing red eyes gazed back at Scarberry as the creature began to stir.

Fearing possible harm, Scarberry quickly stepped on the accelerator and headed the car onto Route 62 in the direction of Point Pleasant, West Virginia. As he drove, one of his passengers began screaming that the strange creature was following them.

A 10-foot (3-meters) wingspan effortlessly enabled the monster to keep up with Scarberry's vehicle. As the creature flew over the car, Mrs. Mallette heard a squeaking sound like that of a mouse. As Scarberry approached the city line, the creature ceased following the vehicle.

Immediately, Scarberry drove to the county sheriff's office and reported what he had seen to Deputy Milland Halstead. Soon the Scarberry-Mallette alien encounter made headlines in newspapers all over the world.

Reported sightings of "Mothman," as the creature was later called, continued through November. "Mothman" became a household name as further sightings of a birdlike creature – 6 to 7 feet (183 to 213 centimeters) tall with glowing red eyes – were reported.

Accompanying the "Mothman" reports were numerous sightings of UFOs in the West Virginia valley from 1966 to the end of 1967.

In December, "Mothman" vanished from West Virginia, but not before more than sixty people reported seeing the strange birdlike creature from November 1966 to December 1967 – more than a year from when it was first sighted.

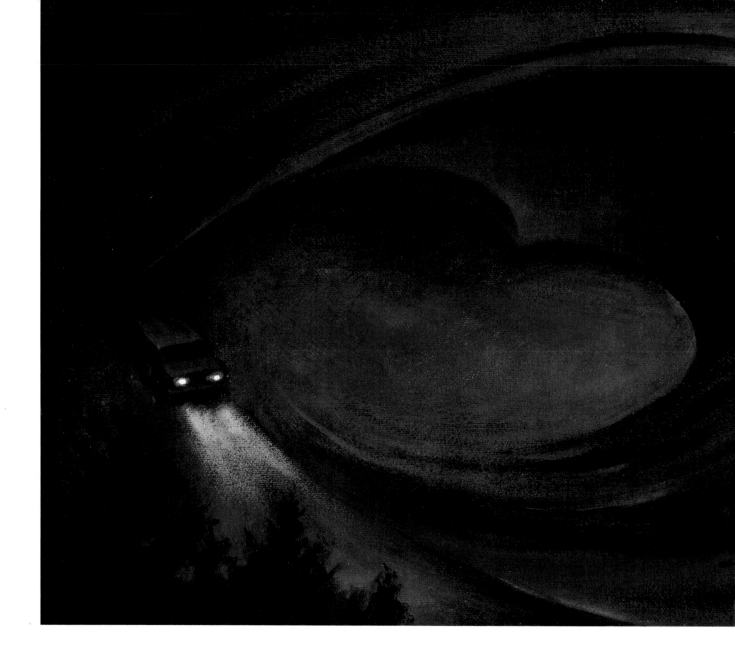

Location of sighting:

Point Pleasant, West Virginia. Not far from an abandoned World War II ammunition dump known as the TNT area. More than sixty other sightings were reported throughout the West Virginia Valley.

Witnesses:

Two couples, Mr. and Mrs. Roger Scarberry and Mr. and Mrs. Steve Mallette, first sighted the creature near the TNT area on November 15, 1966.

Alien

A birdlike creature, gray in color, though some reports described the alien as brown with no discernible arms or legs.

Height: 6 to 7 feet
(183 to 213 centimeters)

Body: Larger than a man in size. No discernible head or arms. Humanlike legs but no feet. Two huge, featherless

wings were tucked under each side
of the figure. Wingspan was between 6
and 10 feet (183 to 300 centimeters).
When leaving the ground or in flight,
the creature's wings were reported not
to flap. Two glowing red eyes about 3
inches (8 centimeters) in diameter were
located in the shoulder area.

Ashland, Nebraska

December 3, 1967

On February 13, 1968, police sergeant Herbert Schirmer, age 22, of Ashland, Nebraska, agreed to let the members of the **University of Colorado UFO Project** investigate, through "time-regression" hypnosis, his reported sighting of December 3, 1967.

The following account of Schirmer's incredible story of an alien abduction is what Schirmer disclosed to the Condon committee.* Prior to this account, Patrolman Schirmer had no recollection of his abduction.

At 2:30 A.M. on December 3, 1967, when Patrolman Schirmer made his usual round of checking on local business establishments, he noticed a football-shaped object, illuminated by pulsating red lights, hovering near the junction of Highways 6 and 63 on the outskirts of Ashland.

As the object began to move away, Schirmer followed in his police cruiser. As he got closer to the object, his car engine and radio went dead.

Within moments, a mysterious-looking figure descended from the alien craft and approached Schirmer's vehicle. Next, the alien pointed an object at the patrol car. A green haze engulfed the area. What Schirmer remembers next is being taken aboard the UFO by a strange-looking creature that he believed to be the commander of the crew.

Aboard the UFO, Schirmer was given a detailed briefing on the reasons that the aliens were observing Earth. He was then instructed on the space vehicle's operation. Following a brief interrogation, Schirmer was directed back to his police cruiser and was told that he would recall nothing of his abduction.

Many UFO investigators believe that the Schirmer incident is still one of the most important cases of alien contact on record.

* The Schirmer abduction is listed as case number 42 in the 1966 Condon Report. This committee was formed and funded by the U. S. Air Force to investigate the possible existence of UFOs.

Craft

Witness: Police sergeant Herbert Schirmer, age 22

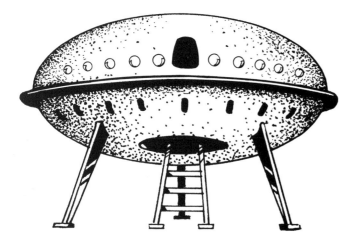

UFO as described by Patrolman Herbert Schirmer on the night of December 3, 1967. He entered the craft by climbing a ladder located at the base.

Descriptions of UFO:

A football-shaped object, approximate 120 feet (36 meters) in diameter, surrounded by flashing red lights. The UFO had a metallic surface that emitted a silver glow, and Schirmer was told by the alien leader that the spaceship was composed of magnesium. A door was located on top of the spacecraft and opened onto a catwalk. Schirmer recalled seeing three legs below the UFO.

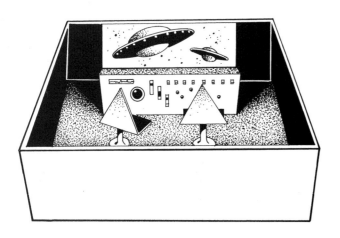

Once inside the UFO, Schirmer was taken into a room that had a large TV-type screen mounted on the wall. Two triangle-shaped chairs were located in front of the screen.

Aboard the UFO, Schirmer remembered being brought into a room approximately 26 feet by 20 feet (8 meters x 6 meters). Lighting in the room gave off a red glow. Two triangle-back chairs in the room stood before a large viewing screen positioned on a wall. On the screen, Schirmer viewed other UFOs. The alien told Schirmer that the UFOs on the screen were enormous "mother ships" floating in deep space. The alien spokesman also told Schirmer that the spaceship he was aboard was an observation craft commanded by a crew of four.

Alien

Schirmer reported seeing a crew of four aliens. The alien who escorted Schirmer aboard the UFO for interrogation was referred to by him as the "leader." All four aliens wore tight-fitting uniforms, boots, and gloves. Their outfits appeared silver in color, and material from their garments was draped over their heads. A small antenna was visible near the area of the aliens' ears.

Height: Approximately 4 to 5 feet (122 to 152 centimeters)

Body: Muscular and human in appearance with flesh white-gray in color

Head and facial features:

Head: Long and thin

Eyes: Catlike in shape with eyebrows that slanted upward

Ears: A small antenna located in the vicinity of the ear

Nose: Large and flat

Mouth: Very thin lips

Imjarvi, Finland

January 7, 1970

Skiing atop the snow-covered slopes around Imjarvi in southern Finland on a beautiful afternoon, Esko Viljo and Aarno Heinonen paused to admire the sunset.

Within moments, the two skiers heard a loud buzzing sound and observed a bright light approaching from the north. Appearing as if it were about to pass directly over their heads, the bright light stopped, and a luminous cloud could be seen rotating around a circular metal object. At the bottom of the object, which appeared to be flat, a tubelike form could be seen protruding from the center. Slowly, the UFO began its descent, stopping just 9 feet above the ground as the two skiers looked on in horror.

Suddenly, a beam of light shot out of the tubelike form, creating a brilliant circle of light, approximately 3 feet (90 centimeters) in diameter, on the freshly fallen snow.

Heinonen was the first to see a skinny creature standing in the beam of light. The creature wore light green overalls and dark green boots. Its face was pale and the color of wax. Clawlike hands held a black box that emitted a yellow pulsating light.

Seconds later, large colorful sparks floated out of the illuminated circle. A thick red mist engulfed the area around the alien, and the light beam slowly began to float upward. When the mist cleared, the alien visitor and UFO had disappeared.

As the two skiers, eager to report what they had seen, began their return to the village, Heinonen fell to the ground. His right side was paralyzed. Viljo helped him down the mountain and to a doctor.

Dr. Pauli Kajanoja examined Heinonen and Viljo and claimed that both skiers had suffered a great shock. Several other people living in the area also reported seeing a bright light in the sky near Imjarvi on the evening of January 7, 1970.

Location of sighting:
An area near the village of Imjarvi in southern Finland

Witnesses:
Farmer Esko Viljo, age 32, and forester Aarno Heinonen, age 36, while skiing the mountain slopes near Imjarvi

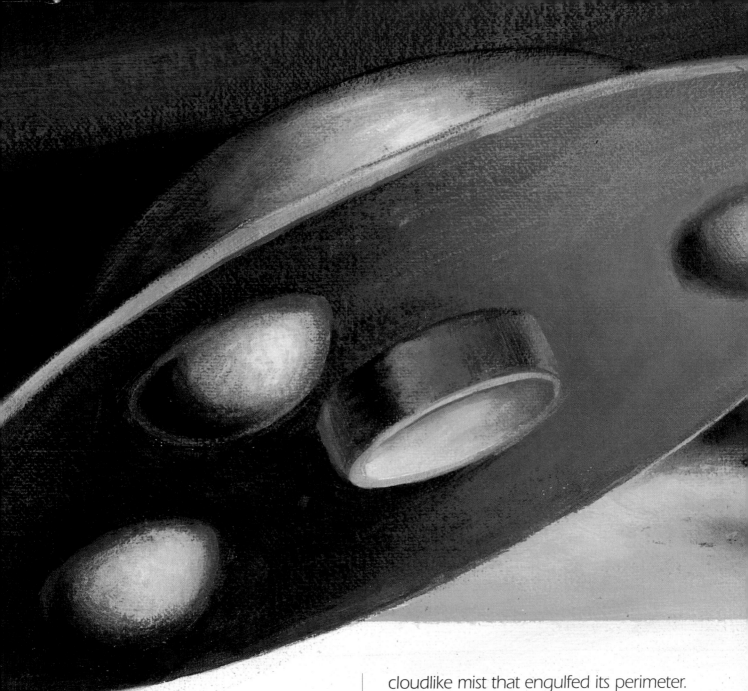

Craft

Descriptions of UFO:

Object first observed as a bright light that emitted a buzzing sound. It appeared saucer-shaped, about 9 to 10 feet (275 to 305 centimeters) in diameter, and surrounded by a red cloudlike mist that engulfed its perimeter. Surface of the UFO appeared to be metal with a flat bottom capped by three hemispheric shapes. A tube protruded from the spacecraft's center and emitted a light that formed an illuminated circle approximately 3 feet (90 centimeters) in diameter on the surface of the snow. Green, red, and purple sparks shot out from the circle of light. Esko and Aarno were struck by some of the flying sparks.

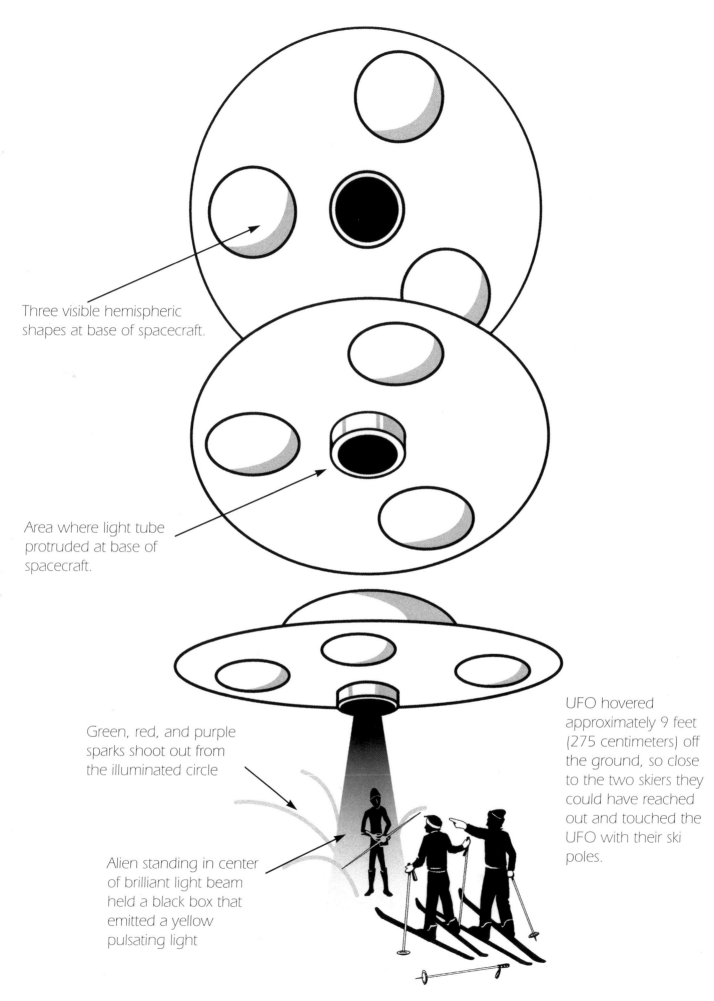

Three visible hemispheric shapes at base of spacecraft.

Area where light tube protruded at base of spacecraft.

Green, red, and purple sparks shoot out from the illuminated circle

Alien standing in center of brilliant light beam held a black box that emitted a yellow pulsating light

UFO hovered approximately 9 feet (275 centimeters) off the ground, so close to the two skiers they could have reached out and touched the UFO with their ski poles.

Alien

Esko Viljo and Aarno Heinonen reported seeing only one alien for approximately twenty seconds before the light beam and alien floated up into the tube that protruded from below the spacecraft.

Height: Approximately 3 feet (90 centimeters)

Body: Alien had a humanlike figure with visible arms and legs. Hands had clawlike fingers that held a black box. The alien wore a tight-fitting, light green suit, dark green boots, and white gloves. Atop the creature's head was a cone-shaped metallic helmet.

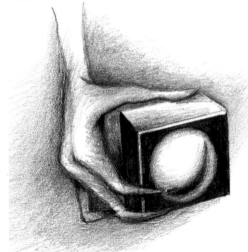

Head and facial features:

Face: Waxlike in color

Eyes: None visible

Nose: Hooklike in shape

Ears: Small and narrow

41

Pascagoula, Mississippi

October 11, 1973

Nothing made for a more relaxing evening than fishing the warm waters near the old shipyard in Pascagoula, Mississippi, and the evening of October 11, 1973, was no exception.

As Charles Hickson and Calvin Parker cast their fishing lines into the water, they spied a bright blue light approaching them from the other side of the river.

Approximately 2 miles (3 kilometers) away, there appeared a football-shaped object in the sky. As the UFO steadily approached and passed over the heads of Charles and Calvin, it hovered above them, about 3 feet (90 centimeters) from the ground.

The craft had a shiny metal surface with blue pulsating lights that seemed to set the whole spacecraft aglow.

Nervously, Calvin pointed to one end of the UFO. As he attempted to draw Charles's attention to that portion of the spacecraft, an opening suddenly appeared in the UFO, and three strange creatures floated out.

Approximately 5 feet (150 centimeters) tall, the creatures looked like wrinkled robots. Their skin or outfits appeared gray in color, and each creature had a head perched atop its shoulders with no visible neck for support. From what Charles and Calvin could see, the nose and ears of the aliens were pointed, and their mouths were small slitlike apertures. No eyes could be seen.

Within moments, two of the aliens floated over to Charles and lifted him off the ground. Slowly, they guided him to the spacecraft.

Upon entering the UFO, Charles noticed that the interior of the vehicle was sparse. No furniture, control panels, or windows could be seen.

One of the aliens slowly pushed Charles backward into a horizontal position. A large piece of machinery, resembling a huge eye, appeared out of nowhere and seemed to be examining or taking an X-ray of Charles. After the examination, the alien gently pushed Charles back into an upright position.

Charles recalled trying to speak to one of the aliens, but the creature responded with a buzzing sound – much like the noise made by a machine. Charles was then sent floating out of the spacecraft and set back on the ground, where he spotted his

friend Calvin standing motionless on the pier. Charles later learned that Calvin had fainted at the sight of the creatures and was also taken aboard the UFO and examined.

Bewildered by their encounter with the aliens, both Charles and Calvin went directly to the police to report what they had experienced.

A UPI press release, printed the day after Charles and Calvin's abduction, reported that the sheriff's office had received numerous calls from Pascagoula residents who claimed they had seen a mysterious glowing oblong object in the sky on the evening of October 11, 1973.

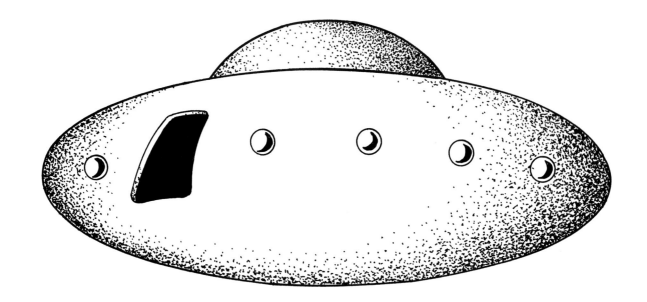

Location of sighting:
The abandoned Shaupeter shipyard in Pascagoula, Mississippi

Witnesses/Abductees:
Shipyard workers Charles Hickson, age 42, and Calvin Parker, age 19, both from Gauther, Mississippi

Craft

Descriptions of UFO:
A large, shiny, metal football-shaped object approximately 10 feet (3 meters) high and 30 feet (9 meters) long, with a visible dome at the top. Pulsating blue lights could be seen on the outside of the vehicle. A door was located at one end of the UFO.

Interior of UFO:
Inside the spacecraft, there was a room equipped for conducting examinations. The room was void of furniture but very well lit. A robotic eye, used for examining objects, seemed to float out from one of the walls and was capable of orbiting an object's perimeter during an examination.

Charles and Calvin reported seeing three aliens float out of an opening in the UFO.

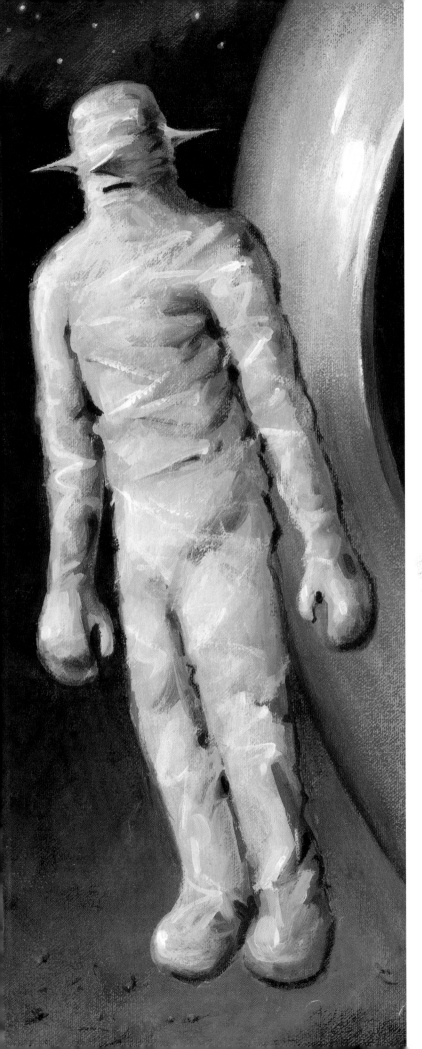

Alien

Both Charles Hickson and Calvin Parker reported seeing three aliens.

Height: Approximately 5 feet (150 centimeters)

Body: Somewhat human in size and structure with gray wrinkled skin. Aliens had long arms, mittenlike hands with a thumb on each hand and feet like an elephant's.

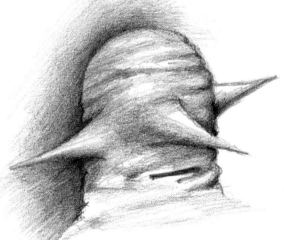

Head and facial features:

Head: Large and perched atop the shoulders without the support of a neck

Eyes: None visible but potentially hidden beneath the wrinkled skin

Ears: Two, long and pointed

Nose: Long and pointed

Mouth: A slit-shaped opening

45

Bibliography

Blum, Ralph and Judy. *Beyond Earth: Man's Contact with UFO's.* New York: Bantam Books, 1974.

Bowen, Charles. *Encounter Cases from Flying Saucer Review.* New York: Signet, 1977.

Clark, Jerome. *The UFO Book: Encyclopedia of the Extraterrestrial.* Detroit: Omnigraphics, 1998.

Edwards, Frank. *Flying Saucers - Serious Business.* New York: Bantam Books, 1966.

Emenegger, Robert. *UFO's Past Present & Future.* New York: Ballantine Books, 1974.

Fuller, John G. *The Interrupted Journey: Two Lost Hours "Aboard a Flying Saucer."* New York: The Dial Press, 1966.

Huyghe, Patrick. *The Field Guide to Extraterrestrials.* New York: Avon Books, 1996.

Hynek, Dr. J. Allen. *The Hynek UFO Report.* New York: Dell Publishing, 1977.

Hynek, Dr. J. Allen. *The UFO Experience, A Scientific Inquiry.* Chicago: Henry Regnery Company, 1972.

Keel, John A. *The Mothman Prophecies.* Avondale Estates, GA: Illuminet Press, 1991.

Norton, Roy. *World's Most Incredible UFO Contact Case (Schirmer Case). Saga,* April 1970.

Randle, Kevin D. *The History of UFO Crashes: Documented Proof of UFO Visits to Earth.* New York: Avon Books, 1995.

Randle, Kevin D. *The Truth About The UFO Crash at Roswell.* New York: M. Evans and Company, 1994.

Randles, Jenny. *Alien Contact: The First Fifty Years.* New York: Sterling Publishing Company, Inc., 1997.

Scientific Study of Unidentified Flying Objects (Condon Report). New York: Bantam Books, 1969.

Spencer, John. *The UFO Encyclopedia.* New York: Avon Books, 1996.

Stanford, Ray. *Socorro "Saucer" in a Pentagon Pantry.* Austin, Texas: Blueapple Books, 1976.

Steiger, Brad. *Alien Meetings.* New York: Ace Books, 1978.

Stringfield, Leonard H. *Situation Red: The UFO Siege.* New York: Fawcett Crest Books, 1977.

The UFO Phenomenon: Mysteries of the Unknown. New York: Time-Life Books, 1987.

Recommended Reading

Clark, Jerome. *The UFO Book: Encyclopedia of the Extraterrestrial.* Detroit: Omnigraphics, 1998.

Darlington, David. *Area 51: The Dreamland Chronicles.* New York: An Owl Book, 1997.

Fiore, Edith, Ph. D. *Encounters: A Psychologist Reveals Case Studies of Abductions by Extraterrestrials.* New York: Ballantine Books, 1997.

Haines, Richard F., Ph.D. *CE-5: Close Encounters of the Fifth Kind.* Naperville, IL: Sourcebooks, Inc., 1999.

Hesemann, Michael. *UFO's: The Secret History.* New York: Marlowe & Company, 1998.

Hynek, Dr. J. Allen. *The UFO Encyclopedia, A Scientific Inquiry.* New York: Marlowe & Company, 1972 (reprint 1998).

Huyghe, Patrick. *The Field Guide to Extraterrestrials.* New York: Avon Books, 1996.

Mannion, Michael. *Project Mindshift.* New York: M. Evans and Company, Inc., 1998.

Pope, Nick. *Open Skies, Closed Minds: For the First Time a Government UFO Expert Speaks Out.* New York: The Overlook Press, 1998.

Randle, Kevin. *The Randle Report: UFO's in the '90s.* New York: M. Evans & Company, Inc., 1997.

Randle, Kevin, and Estes, Russ. *Faces of the Visitors: An Illustrated Reference to Alien Contact.* New York: Simon & Schuster, 1997.

Randles, Jenny. *UFO Retrievals: The Recovery of Alien Spacecraft.* London: A Blandford Book, 1995.

Randles, Jenny. *Alien Contact: The First Fifty Years.* New York: Sterling Publishing Company, 1997.

Spencer, John. *The UFO Encyclopedia.* New York: Anon Books, 1996.

Strieber, Whitney. *Communion.* New York: Avon Books, Inc., 1987.

Walton, Travis. *Fire in the Sky.* New York: Marlowe & Company, 1979.

Yenne, Bill. *U.F.O. Evaluating the Evidence.* New York: Smithmark Books, 1997.

About the Author

Peter A. Campbell is a 1970 graduate of Vesper George School of Art, Boston, Massachusetts. His paintings have been exhibited throughout the East Coast and are represented in many private collections. He has won over twenty painting awards and honors, including membership in the National Society of Painters in Casein and Acrylic in New York City. Peter is also a member of the Society of Children's Book Writers and Illustrators.

Photograph: Gene Dwiggins

In 1988, Peter was selected by NASA to become a member of its space art program. This program documents major aerospace activities by recording them in artwork.

In 1989, he spent a week touring, sketching, and photographing the activities at the Kennedy Space Center in Florida. He also witnessed the exciting launch of the space shuttle *Atlantis*, which carried the Venus probe Magellan. From this experience Peter created the painting "Voyage to Venus," which now hangs in NASA's permanent art collection in Florida. Peter's space paintings have also been featured in *The Artist* magazine.

In 1995, Millbrook published Peter's first children's book titled *Launch Day,* which he wrote and illustrated.

He has also worked as an art director and creative director for several Rhode Island advertising agencies. Peter lives in Lincoln, Rhode Island, with his wife Karen and their three sons Seth, Jeremy, and Brendan.